CHIARA MASON

CHIARA MASON
Blooming: Poetry for Seasons of Change

Published by Chiara Mason
Copyright © 2023 by Chiara Mason
First Edition

Paperback ISBN   978-1-7388161-2-5
eBook ISBN   978-1-7388161-0-1

All rights reserved under International and Pan-American Copyright Conventions. Manufactured in Canada.

No part of this publication may be reproduced, stored in or introduced into a retrieval system, or transmitted in any form or by any means (electronic, mechanical, photocopying, recording or otherwise) without prior permission of the publisher. This book is sold subject to the condition that it will not, by way of trade or otherwise, be lent, resold, hired out, or otherwise circulated without the publisher's prior written consent, in any way binding, cover or condition other than that in which it was published.

Cover & Book Design: Tracy Hetherington
Bio Photography Credit: Kayley Bourcier
Editing: Elise Volkman
Publishing Support: TSPA The Self Publishing Agency Inc.

For TS — I hope you're flying high on angel wings.

For those who are struggling — you are not alone. XO

Contents

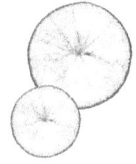

SOLSTICE 1

SUMMER 5
FALL 45
WINTER 89
SPRING 131

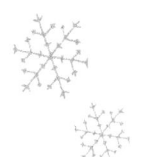

EQUINOX 167

Solstice

Growing up, we're taught all of these values that we tend to carry with us for a long time. Inevitably, we reach a crossroads where these values are put to the test. We're pushed to see how and when we will cave to something that doesn't align with who we are.

But what happens when you don't need a test for that to happen? When you wind up coming to question those values all on your own—and the very root of it, who you are at your core?

Somewhere between my lone wanderings—new friendships, nights spent laughing in hotel rooms in foreign cities, endless sangria, delicious food, allergic reactions, getting lost and found, dying in insane heat, running around new cities intoxicated, admiring architecture and artwork, exploring new places and discovering new things—it hit me that I had been lying to myself. For a while. Because of that, I was no longer myself. And that was a big, big problem.

It can be incredibly difficult to move forward when you don't know who you want to be in the future. What kind of person you want to be. You question if it's necessary to stay on the straight and narrow all the time. You know you can make mistakes, but what happens when those mistakes wind up defining who you are as a person? There are some things you can't come back from. Some things change everything.

So who is it that you want to be? Who do you want to become? And how do the choices you make get you there?

Sometimes we need to move forward. Sometimes we have to say goodbye in order to say hello to bigger and better things. Yes, that's a cliché, but it's a true one. However, that doesn't mean it's easy. It's really fucking hard.

Saying goodbye to some place or someone that makes you feel safe and taking the chance on something or someone else—running the risk of getting hurt or not making it or failing—is very hard. But you will never know if you never try.

Maybe you'll be rewarded and meet the love of your life, or find what you're truly passionate about, or make an incredible discovery about yourself.

Or maybe it will be a total disaster and you'll end up broke and broken hearted, a failure feeling utterly lost.

Either way, it will be worth it. Because you tried and you gave it your all.

In the end, all of these experiences make us who we are. The mistakes, the heartbreaks, the almost-in-debt or the in-debt, the love, the hurt, the happiness, the feeling of growth, the feeling of accomplishment, the feeling of being yourself and being fulfilled and knowing that *that is enough*. It all makes us who we are. And eventually, everything will fall into place. Then you'll know. You'll know that it was all worth it.

Or maybe you'll never know.

Maybe you'll always be uncertain, and questioning, and trying, and failing, and getting up again, and succeeding, and falling down again, and repeating it over and over and over.

Because that's life: uncertainty, not knowing if things will work out but trying your best anyway. It's worrying that you'll make the wrong choice, but knowing in your heart that you have to try. It's being afraid that you won't be enough, but having enough faith to push yourself to despite your doubts. You never know what will happen next. Change will always come your way. So embrace it. Be grateful for it. Trust it. It will lead you on the path you were meant to be on in this crazy wild ride that is life.

The thing about finding your way is that many things will try to get in your way. The thing about becoming who you are meant to be is that some people don't want to see your light shine. But you can't let that hold you back. You have to reach for what you want and live your best life. You have to move forward and let go of what is no longer positively impacting you.

If someone is not contributing to your happiness and lifting you up, let them go.

If you're in a place that causes you more harm than good, no matter how good the good might be, let it go.

If someone disrupts your sense of who you are for their own benefit, let them go.

If you surround yourself with only the negatives and never the positives, let them go.

If someone disrespects you in any way, whether they're family or friends or lovers, let them go.

If the people in your life are not supporting you and making you feel loved and fulfilled, let them go.

If you are forcing yourself to do something that doesn't actually make you feel *alive*, let it go.

You will find the people that you need. You will find the path that is meant to be yours. And, ultimately, the most important person that you need is yourself.

If you're reading this, I hope you're not putting too much insane pressure on yourself to live up to expectations and be perfect—even if those expectations are entirely self-inflicted. No matter where you're at or how you're doing right now, you can do this, and you will do it in your own wonderfully imperfect and unique way.

Summer

Blooming: Poetry for Seasons of Change

Summer

All of a sudden, my life started to change.

There was a bend in the road,

And I had no idea what it was going to bring.

But we need to make the best of life, whether it's good or bad,

Because the bends in the road will keep coming—that's life.

In the beginning, it all seems so simple;

Everything is easy and comes so naturally.

It's hard to imagine a time in which things are difficult,

In which things could change,

In which things could ever be different than how they are right now,

in this moment.

You think about all of the moments that

seem to be slipping away,

Before you can fully grasp them.

And yet, right now,

You are living it,

And enjoying it,

And not knowing how desperately you will later be wishing

That you could get these moments back.

Summer

Suddenly it just hit me, like lightning when it strikes;

Struck me so hard, it didn't even seem real.

Just thinking about you makes me smile.

I feel like you know the real me, not the one I try to show everybody else.

You showed me that I can't be anybody else but me;

I'm falling for you.

Grey clouds breaking away;

The sun is shining, you're the light of my day.

Bright blue sky's stretching 'cross the horizon,

And I'll wait for you…

Summer

A beautiful outdoor paradise

Exploration at every corner

Delicious wine and food at your fingertips

Amazing views at every turn

Fueled by tourism

Retirement destination

Entrepreneurial spirit

Growing and changing

My home

–The Okanagan

I still find it odd

How those things I used to think were so funny

Just aren't funny anymore.

I don't know if I'm growing up or if I'm just changing,

But I know that I can't stay this way.

The growth I had during that time has pushed me to today.

It has pushed me to fight for me and to be strong for what I believe in;

To never give up on what I want.

I know that I can make a difference in this world

As long as I keep trying…

I am spinning in circles

And the world moves around me

Spinning and spinning out of control

I see no end in sight

Everything is a mess

I don't know how to get back on track

Or if I even want to get back on track

–*It's all a mess*

Nothing feels certain anymore.

For so long, I had it in my head that I had to be a certain way, accomplish certain things, have certain goals. But suddenly it feels so foreign and unlike me. What is the point of it all? What is my purpose for being here?

It's so hard when you feel like you don't have a purpose. There's nothing pushing you forward, nothing begging you to stay, nothing to fight for.

I want to find my purpose. I need one to keep me moving forward. But it's difficult. Some days I just feel so lost. I have nowhere to turn and no idea where the road will take me.

The uncertainty is killing me. Where do I even begin?

Summer

I'm so scared and I don't know what to do

Or where to go from here

Or what is going to happen next

How much do you have to sacrifice

In order to achieve greatness?

When does it stop?

Summer

I feel like

I don't really know who I am

And it's making me kind of sad

—*The blues*

What is the point

In existing?

I know that everything happens for a reason,

But damn,

It's killing me.

Summer

What is the answer?

Perhaps there isn't one

And it's just up to us to enjoy what we have while we have it.

Time management has never been my strong suit.

It's difficult when everyone is pulling you in different directions. Achieving balance is something I find challenging.

I have to balance my career with my relationships.

I have to balance my desire to be uncommitted, unsettled and free—travelling the world—with my equal desire for stability and a career.

I have to balance my desire to be loved with my desire to be a strong and independent woman who is fine on her own.

I have to balance my own desires with the desires of others, who think they know me better than I know myself.

I have to balance my own happiness with the feelings of others.

Where do I draw the line? At what point do these competing demands win against one another? What about my *own* happiness?

Maybe it would be easier if I didn't care. If I could just pick a side. But that's the point of having to balance it all—you have so many different aspects that you care about, you simply can't pick just *one*. You need to find a way to balance them *all*.

Question is…

How?

Summer

What happens when you feel like

You are being

P   u   l   l   e   d

In multiple directions?

What do you choose?

What about the direction that *I* want?

When there is so much going on in your head,

It can be difficult to separate it all and find what really matters.

How is it that I can make so many mistakes?
That I can love the most amazing person in the universe, and then you come along, and my universe is somehow shifted?
How is it that you can make no one else matter anymore?

That all the others before, I still love, but for you, I would die.
How is it that I can be so blindsided by someone's desire—so much so that I fall for them and forget about you?
How could I let that happen?
How could I ever forget you?

How is it that this is taking so long?
That you do not see what I've been trying to hide for so long?

I can meet someone who is the sweetest person in the universe, who would love to be with me, yet I look in your eyes and know that I can't.

I choose you over them; I choose you over everyone…

"Why," you ask, "is it always you?"
Trust me when I say:
I've asked myself the exact same thing way too many times.
Trying to draw a logical explanation as to why it is you—
Why it is always going to be you—
Why I can't be with anyone else no matter how badly I want to.

Because I need to be with you—
It is almost beyond my understanding…
It is love.

Things are always more complex than they may seem. You never know what someone is truly going through.

I'm sure that I'm not the only one who has had these feelings at some point. Some days, my heart feels so happy and full of love. Other days, I sit on my bedroom floor and cry for a long time.

I am working on accepting the contradictions in my life and in myself, and trying my best to express them in a way that is honest and real. Being as open as I can is the best I can do.

It's hard to do everything on your own.

These days, we have so many responsibilities.

It would be easier to ignore them and follow a life of pure bliss and pleasure,

But I suppose that's unrealistic.

Damn, being an adult is hard.

Wasn't all of this easier when we were kids?

What happens when you come to a situation in which you are faced with deciding between something you *should* do and something you *want* to do?

I know that I should make smart decisions that will advance my career: protect my finances, protect my heart, stay on the safe side of things, maintain relationships with family members.

But that doesn't mean I always want to do these things.

Sometimes I feel so torn. Sometimes I want to be reckless and take a chance on something that might not work out—take a risk. Sometimes I don't want to force myself into situations that feel heavy and full of obligation rather than happiness.

Sometimes I just want to follow my heart.

I wish it was simple and we could just pick a side. But life isn't that simple. I guess it's all about compromise.

What happens when the compromise leaves you completely unhappy?

All I truly want is to be happy. Some days it feels so far away that I fear I may never reach it.

Summer

When you finally get

What you thought would make you happy

And suddenly…

You're not.

Then you can't help but think…

Now what?

I don't know what I'm doing;

I don't really know why I'm back here.

But I know that it all happens for a reason.

We're slowly slipping back into our old routine.

I'm thinking I just might be falling for you,

And I don't want to over-anticipate,

But I'm thinking you might be falling for me too.

Can't you see?

You're the only one who can, who has, who will

Come between us—

Who destroyed us—

Who yet still destroys me—

Simply because you do not see.

The world is pushing me back toward you

And I can't fight this feeling;

I need you, and we've only got so long left.

I wish you could see it;

I wish you could feel what I do when I look into your eyes…

Why can't you see?

You're perfect for me, and I for you.

Those eyes bring me back to you every time—

They won't let me go

I can't let you go

Please don't let me go…

You're looking at me with those intense eyes,

Smiling and laughing like we've known each other our whole lives

And I feel something stirring inside of me;

I can't take my eyes off your face…

I've never felt anything like this before;

You're the only thing on my mind.

I never thought I'd feel like I've finally found the one

And I feel something stirring inside of me;

A connection that's impossible to break…

We're ignoring the dirty looks other people give us

And when they talk, we pretend we don't hear.

There are so many coincidences—maybe fate brought us together

And I feel something stirring inside of me;

I don't know if I could survive without you in my life.

Things that I really struggle with:

- Need to love
- Self confidence + acceptance + love
- Being healthy
- Connection vs. independence
- Sex drive
- Maintaining friendships
- Grieving TS
- How to balance it all
- Myself vs. loved ones
- Travelling vs. a stable career

I never wanted to fall for you

But when it started to happen, I knew I couldn't fight it.

Little did I know how a simple feeling

could turn into something so much bigger…

What they didn't know

Is how we understood each other in a way no one else did.

Even though things have changed,

I still wish I had you.

I used to be so bold and confident—

Not afraid to do what I want and say what I feel!

Where did all of that go?

Suddenly, nothing makes sense anymore.

Should I change all of my qualities?

Do I even enjoy the work I am doing?

Do I enjoy the connections I have?

Are my ultimate goals in life changing,

Or maybe a better question is,

Should they change?

Things I once used to be so sure of, I'm not anymore.

Everything feels different, and nothing feels the same.

With all of these questions and everything up in the air,

I'm not sure where to go from here.

Who do I want to be?

What values do I want to embody?

How do the decisions I make

Affect the rest of my life?

Where do I draw the line?

Is it okay to pursue only what *I* want

And only do what makes *me* happy?

All of these questions…

They need answers.

–I can't find the answers

I wish I didn't feel like I have to choose

Between growth and self development and empowerment and having my shit together,

Or breaking down and crying; being emotional and feeling my feelings, and acting out 'cause I want to; being a little slutty and a little unstable.

Why do I feel like there is such a big divide between being "put together"

And being a hot mess?

Why can't I be both?

Or why can't I be one or the other when I feel like it?

I don't want to feel like I need to have it together all the time and always be moving forward. Because sometimes, *a lot of the time,*

I don't. And I don't want to feel guilty for taking time to myself, to feel and do what I want without necessarily moving forward in that moment.

I don't always want to be looking for the next thing to improve.

I want to be in the now and feel *every moment,*

Even the ones that hurt so bad, I feel like I might never get pieced back together again.

The overwhelming amount of pressure we put on ourselves

To live up to constructed expectations

Is just insane.

Yet there's something that keeps pushing me to try and obtain them.

Maybe it would be easier if I just didn't care,

But I do.

This pushes me to strive harder,

And when I don't reach these achievements,

I feel like I have failed.

We can't possibly do it all.

Sometimes we focus so much on making things seem like they're perfect

When they actually aren't.

Sometimes, they are so far from it.

And yet we push ourselves to try to fit this "perfection,"

Even though we know

We will never fully reach it.

–*Perfection is an illusion*

You're still on my mind, like you have been for three months…

I wonder, will this ever stop?

How many times will I fall for you?

How many times will you break my heart?

How many times will I gaze into those beautiful eyes?

Now I don't know if I'll be able to get myself out of this mess;

How many times can I tell you I'm sorry?

How can this be wrong if it feels so right?

I know it's wrong, but that makes me want you even more…

I want you more than I've ever wanted anything.

I want you to make me scream

In the best possible way.

I want to connect with you on every level,

Until we become one.

Summer

Being with you

Is paradise

Your lips touch mine

And nothing else matters.

The world fades away

And it's just you and me.

–Bliss

Summer

You make love feel

As easy as breathing

Never thought this was going to happen;
Never thought we'd end up like this.
It's been a crazy ride but we still made it.

Never thought I'd find love that's like a fairytale—
So magical and breathtaking, captivating, heart stopping,
It makes life feel complete when I'm with you.
I think this was meant to happen, so let's run away.

I know you can save me.
I've been waiting to find you and I've finally found the one,
So don't hold back.
Let's fulfill our fairytale and find our happy ending.

Now look where we're at—
We've become very good friends and I am so glad.
I'm crazy about you and sometimes
I still have to pinch myself because I can't believe this is happening.
I am so lucky that I found you;
I hope you never leave…

This is my promise to you:
We're going to make it,
No matter what.
We will find a way
'Cause I would cross oceans for you and I know you would do the same.
So let's not wait; let's start today.

Fall

Blooming: Poetry for Seasons of Change

I think you saved me and broke me at the same time.

When my life is slipping out of control,

And I'm feeling like I've got nowhere to go,

And I'm almost breaking down…

I need you right now.

Can someone tell me why I feel this way?

Why is life so confusing?

The way I feel about you is driving me crazy.

I just don't know what to do.

When will I figure things out?

Someday I'll realize that I need to snap out of it;

Someday I'll wake up and finally start living my life right.

It's just so confusing and I've got no one to turn to.

I don't understand why I'm feeling this way.

I know someday things will all make sense…

Can you tell me, when is someday?

It was like someone slapped a door in my face,

Told me to wake up, and take a serious look at my life.

Why wasn't I happy?

I genuinely thought that what I had been doing would make me happy.

Even more than that, I *convinced* myself that these things made me happy.

Clearly, that wasn't the case.

Fall

The older I get, the harder things are,

And the more I wish things could be simple again.

Back when I had you, my life seemed complete.

But with everything that has happened, now it all seems off.

If only things were simple again, this would be easy…

Lately, I've been feeling so lost.

Every decision I make feels like the wrong choice.

I can't seem to find a clear path forward.

Instead of certainty, I feel like I'm in a maze;

Thousands of directions that I could go,

And I have no *idea* which road to take.

It feels like I don't even know myself;

I want to get her back, but I don't know how.

The circle of all the harmonious aspects of our relationship

Is broken.

I know it was my fault,

But what do I do now?

The last of it is barely staying together.

I don't know what to do or say to fix this,

Or if I even can fix this,

Or if I even want to.

Do you want to?

It feels like up is down and down is up

Everything is turned around and upside down

–Grief

Fall

I don't know if I can do this anymore…

Why can't we make this work?

Why can't the stars align and

For once in my life,

Why can't things turn out right?

The seasons change and so do I,

but I wish we could have stayed the same.

Fall

Seeing you with them kills me.

You flirt and talk with them, and it kills me.

I try to act like everything is okay,

Try to make it through another day,

But each day is harder than the last—

And it kills me.

I have a habit of running

When things start going downhill.

I would rather *run*

Than face the consequences.

Now I can't stop running

Maybe I'm scared that, if I stop moving, everything around me will stop—

And come c
        r
          a
            s
              h
                i
                  n
                    g
                      down

Fall

All of this confusion is too much.

The chaos outside of your life has started to move inside of your head, and you can't seem to escape it. There's nothing left to do but run away. You can't wait to escape it all. You have never wanted to leave this life so badly and get away from all of the chaos. The relationships, the uncertainty, the fragmentation—leaving it all behind sounds like perfection.

I'll run with you. I won't leave you to suffer this alone. Running away sometimes seems like the answer, but you can't escape everything. You need someone to support you through this difficult time.

Now you can't wait to leave it all behind. You start running and you never stop. Stopping means looking back at everything you've left behind. Stopping means letting it all soak in. Stopping means taking accountability for everything that has happened. You aren't ready to do that just yet.

So you keep running, hoping that, eventually, if you run far enough, it will all fade away. You won't have to look back because it will be so far behind you, that you can barely glimpse it anymore. You won't have to accept any responsibility if you just keep moving.

If you leave it all behind, maybe—just maybe—the past will never catch up to you. And maybe you can forget it ever happened…

But what happens if the running doesn't help?

We can't run forever.

The world around me is spinning; moving in circles. Everyone seems to be getting their shit together, getting their lives on track.

And me? I'm frozen. Stuck in place. Incapable of moving, growing, or changing.

I am stuck on this life trajectory. Even if I wanted to make a change, I know that I can't.

I feel so trapped. I don't know how to get out of the mess that I have created. Just because it wasn't *all* my fault doesn't mean that *some* of the blame shouldn't fall on me. This was my own disaster, and I was destined to sit in it.

I can't break free. I'm not a bird that can fly up and out of here. At this point, I'm more like a tree. My roots are in deep, getting deeper by the day, and I can't just uproot myself and find somewhere else to be.

This is my fate. I have made my bed; it's time to lie in it.

Fall

I'm in quicksand.

This isn't what I want,

But, somehow, here I am.

I don't know how to get *out*—

And that is terrifying.

Maybe I am too worried about what others will think.

What happened to doing things for me?

To making my own choices because that's what feels good?

Somehow, I am stuck in the now.

I can't seem to make my next move.

You saved me when I was in desperate need of saving.

When everything else was falling apart,

You were there to catch me—

To keep me afloat when I felt like I was drowning.

And then, I got used to you.

Suddenly, I felt like I could never stay afloat unless you were there.

I need you, desperately.

You're my life raft; you keep me going when the waves get choppy.

I wish I could have been who you needed me to be.

I wish I didn't change with the seasons.

I wish we could grow and change together,

But it's not so.

I wish it was different.

I'm sorry.

I wish it was easier for me to make decisions.

I wish I could purely pursue what I want,

Without worrying about what others will think.

For some reason, I can't turn off that part of my brain.

What if everyone disagrees with me?

What if they all stop talking to me?

What if I lose them?

I am *so* scared of that happening,

And I can't make that fear go away.

Vulnerability is a virtue and a blessing

Not something to be afraid of

I keep getting that feeling,

And I haven't felt this way in such a long time…

I keep telling myself to give it up,

but I can't—

I can't give you up—

I have to try.

How can you miss someone you don't even know?

I don't think I'll ever stop missing you.

I don't think I'll ever love anyone the way I loved you.

Fall

Some people might ask:

If I knew I'd be hurt, why did I bother in the first place?

Truth is, I knew I had to take the chance.

I knew you'd be worth it;

I knew that I would learn so much from you.

They want me to give it up,

But in all honesty, I'd rather be with you now

And get hurt later on,

Than not get to be with you at all.

You're worth the hurt.

I'll fight, fight, fight until I get what I want.

Why can't you see the passion that's burning through me?

They think if they tell me to give it up, I will, but they're wrong.

I have the drive, and when I want something, I'll fight for it.

And I want you.

I need to fight until the end, and even if you change your mind,

I know it will all have been worth it,

'Cause I was cared for by someone as amazing as you.

I can't explain it, but with you, it's different.

When I'm with you, my heart starts to beat fast;

Seeing you smile makes me the happiest person in the world.

And then there's the question:

Should I stay and fight for you,

Or should I keep it all locked up inside, and go back to us being best friends

And forget this growing feeling that I keep getting towards you?

I know it's a bad thing, to depend on someone this much.

But I just can't help it.

You mean so much to me and I need you in my life.

I am looking for love because I've been in it before,

And it's the most powerful feeling in the universe.

I've always been giving out love, and now all I ask is something in return…

Maybe you'll realize that you were wrong, that we could've worked it out,

'Cause I loved you with all my heart, but you didn't know.

I don't understand how your brain twisted what we are—

No, I don't understand

How something that feels so right could suddenly go wrong.

I thought we had more, but I guess you thought differently.

You told me you loved me, but now I see that you don't.

You've kissed me, held me, embraced me,

Pampered me, showed me off…

Was that all a silly game?

I actually thought that this was something different;

I actually suspected that this time it was real.

I guess I was wrong—clearly it isn't real in your eyes…

Why did you say you loved me if you didn't mean it?

Love resembles a fairytale,

'Cause fairytales don't come true.

Think I'm done fighting…

Maybe now it's time to give up.

Things have gotten so complicated,

That I am now always unsure of what to say,

How to act,

How to feel.

I need to tread lightly.

I don't know how to approach you.

I don't know if I should be trying to fix this or not,

Because I truly can't tell how invested you are in this relationship.

I don't know how much to say,

Because I don't want to push your buttons

And wind up pushing you away.

I want this to work, but do you?

I need to give you an ultimatum. I am worried that we are at the tipping point.

You know that I have made some choices about my future recently that are big. And I am not sure how you feel about them.

Though I love you, I think we need to make a choice. I don't want to stay together, if you're hoping for things that I can't promise. I can't promise you stability in anything. I can't promise where I am going to wind up living, what I am going to wind up doing, when I am going to settle down, or even if I want to. I don't want you holding on to false hope, and I want you to achieve everything you want in life.

I think you need to consider what you really want. Is it me? Or is it settling down in a quiet place with someone, doing the same things all the time? Because that isn't me. And I can't promise that it will ever be me.

So it's time for you to make a choice.

Fall

I couldn't fall asleep because the rain was slamming against my window last night.

I wish it could've drowned out my thoughts of you—

But it didn't.

Damn it.

Wouldn't it be easier if feelings could wash away like dirt on the sidewalk?

I am scared to let you go.

What if I can't make it on my own?

Fall

You were my life raft;

I needed you to survive.

But maybe it's time

To try swimming on my own.

I've got a rep for messing things up,

And now I've messed them up with you.

I didn't mean to, didn't try to, don't really know why you won't talk to me…

Remember how we talked about that person we were missing?

The one who would make our world stop spinning?

The one who would change everything?

I've been thinking, should I give up on you and search for them instead?

Could I leave you? Should I leave you?

Somehow, I have to…

What kills me the most

Is that you don't try to stop me

When I finally decide

To walk away.

I know that I need to make a change;

I can feel it in my bones.

But I am fucking terrified of what will come next—

Mostly because I have *no fucking clue* what that will be.

I'm scared to mess everything up with you. It's been a while since something has felt like it's going right in my life. And now that I'm finally there, I don't want it all to slip away.

What if I say the wrong thing? What if I make the wrong move at the wrong time? What if I lose it all? Everything feels so delicate. One false step feels like it could send everything crashing down.

These are the things I have worked so hard for: relationships I've created, a career I've built, and progress I've made in so many other areas of my life. Yet, somehow, it feels like it's all on the line—that my entire world could shatter at any second.

Maybe that's the point. Maybe we will never be able to know that we won't mess things up. Maybe we just need to keep trying not to.

And if it does all come crashing down… maybe it was meant to.

I am at the precipice of a big decision.

I know which route I want to take

And what it could potentially give me—

Happiness, freedom, flexibility.

But I am also very aware of what I will be giving up:

Stability, safety, consistency.

What if I make the wrong choice?

Am I crazy for wanting to pursue something different?

What if I do pursue it, and I mess up everything?

I don't want to mess it all up.

But I also don't want to stay where I am.

I'm infused with mixed feelings and I'm not sure which road to take.

I wish I had more certainty, but all I feel is confusion and chaos.

Making this decision was not easy.

It was the hardest decision I have ever made.

I question every single day whether it was the right choice.

Since then, a lot more has happened,

And lately, I feel that I've been wrecking pretty much everything I touch.

I struggle with placing the blame on myself.

I try to believe that everything happens for a reason,

But, sometimes, that's a hard pill to swallow.

Fall

I'm so afraid of whether or not

Everything is going to work out.

I keep telling myself that it will—

That it has to,

That this life will never be over until it is all worked out—

But what if it doesn't?

I've forever been plagued by the fear that I'm not good enough

That I always need to keep pushing myself for more

And if I make one false move, and mess up

Then suddenly I won't be worthy anymore

Things that I'm afraid of messing up:

- Graduation, even though I'm so close
- My future career
- Family relationships
- Friendships that grow apart because of distance
- My health and wellbeing
- My finances/savings
- Failing to critically think about the world around me
- Anything with you

I wish there was a way

I could fix it all;

Make sure everything will work out

And be okay.

But I wouldn't even know where to start.

Here's hoping.

Winter

Blooming: Poetry for Seasons of Change

It has taken me a long time to figure out just how much of a fucking disaster this relationship is. I never realized before how you fail to support me.

You do not celebrate my achievements, or even ask how things are going in my life. You only seek to even have a relationship with me when it's convenient for you. And every time I share something, you try to one-up me. It seems like you're only interested in my downfalls and failures. Are you just laughing at me behind my back?

A relationship is meant to be two people supporting one another and lifting each other up, in the good and the bad. That is not what this is. This reeks of toxicity, guilt, pettiness, and shame. And somehow all of these feelings get pushed onto me.

I don't know why it took me so long to realize how heavy this relationship makes me feel—and unsatisfied, and generally unhappy.

If that is all true, then it should be easy to let you go. To walk away. To leave it all behind...

I wish it were that simple.

Was it all in my head?

Was I just being used?

Did I not see the signs?

Did I push you too hard?

Was I not clear enough?

Do I want you to be a stranger?

How do I move forward now?

It's hard to believe that it's over;

I keep thinking you'll text me just like before.

Things have been rough.

Last night, I found myself crying on my bedroom floor.

It's been a while since that has happened—

I truly was not anticipating everything to hit me with such full force.

–Rough nights

The pain is excruciating—and then nothing.

It feels as if it didn't happen at all.

Losing you is my nightmare.

Winter

You gave me sunshine,

But eventually

It poured.

I lost it all,

And worse still:

I had to let you go.

Letting go of someone you love is the worst feeling in the world.

It's like a part of you gets ripped out...

I can't breathe.

Letting go of you is so hard, I don't quite know exactly what to be when you're not around.

I need to let go of everything that we've been through;

I need to look forward and not back;

I need to forget the past and keep my eyes ahead.

I know everything happens for a reason.

One day you'll regret letting me walk away,

But, right now, it's my turn to say goodbye

And let you go.

I don't know how I will ever get past this.

I don't know if I'll ever have those feelings again.

I'm still dreaming that you'll change your mind and come around.

How am I supposed to forget you when I never really had you?

How do I find a way to move on when it was never really real?

But damn, it felt real. I felt it.

What happens when you're all that I can think about?

I wish I could erase you from my memory and get a blank slate.

What if I don't want to be friends?
I don't know if I can.
Oh my god, it hurts so bad—
I didn't think it was possible to feel this hurt again.
I don't want to feel hurt, I want to feel numb.

I wish they could go away and I could turn them off,
But feelings don't have a switch
And me continuing to talk to you isn't going to help.
I just don't know where to go from here.

I feel so confused—
Sick to my stomach and I can't sleep.
You would think, because I now have an answer from you, it would make things easier.
But it hasn't really.

Because how can I move on from you when I so clearly saw it?
I made up so many things in my head and now…
I don't know how to make it stop.
I didn't think I would have to deal with this situation again.
I just don't know how to move on.

Even though I know that this is not a good relationship,
Even though I know you are a bad influence on me,
Even though I know we have nothing in common,
Even though I know we want different things,
Even though I know I should feel light and happy when I'm with you, and I don't,
Even though I know we have grown apart over time…
I somehow can't find it in me to let you go.

I still have feelings for you that won't go away.
I have invested so much time and energy into this relationship
And I don't want to lose it.
I still know that you care about me.
I still know that you are family, and that is not something you walk away from.
I still know that you want this relationship in your life.
I still know that we could find a way to work, if we really wanted to.
I still know that you are the love of my life.
And yet, despite it all, I don't want to let you go.

I would do anything to have things go back to the way they were,
Before it all fell apart.
But this isn't healthy anymore.
Even though I don't want to…
I have to let you go.

The places that tore on my heartstrings until I fell apart:

- Kelowna
- Manchester
- Our first apartment
- The running track near our place
- Walking on eggshells at my old school
- Being surrounded by people I know, yet feeling more alone than ever

You were my entire universe.

I know that I've said it sucks to depend on someone this much,

So from this day forward, I won't anymore.

Yes, I love you with all of my heart, but I can't be the only one fighting all the time.

It's not fair for me to get that broken down when you suddenly decide not to talk to me.

It's not cool for you to ignore me and pretend that I don't exist.

Do I really mean that little to you?

So little that you can't even acknowledge that I'm there?

Can't even bother to look at me, let alone talk to me?

Well, guess what? I'm done. I can't deal with it anymore.

You're not going to be my whole world.

You can't be, because there is so much more in this world besides you and I.

If you're not going to treat me the way I deserve to be treated, then I'm breaking free.

I'm leaving today.

I never thought it would hurt so bad. I mean, I knew that it would hurt. I didn't want to let you go, but I had to, for the sake of both of us. We just weren't working anymore in a way that was productive, meaningful, or healthy.

But, damn. That didn't make it easy.

It hurts like hell. It feels like every piece of my body is shattering into a million pieces. It feels like I can never go anywhere easily again, because I'm scared of running into you. To have to see your face. To face what happened. To see the hurt in your eyes.

It feels like part of me is gone; like I will never be whole again. It would be so much easier if I had stayed—if I had tried just one more time. But I've tried over and over and over and I'm exhausted. I can't do it anymore. I thought that, if I said goodbye, the hurt would stop. But it didn't. It just got worse.

I don't know if the pain of letting you go will ever go away. I know that it was my choice. But that doesn't mean it was an easy choice. It was the hardest decision of my life, and for a long time, I questioned if I did the right thing.

But I know in my heart this is what is best for all of us.

It hurts like hell. Sometimes it is necessary to hurt to move on. Unfortunately, I don't know when that will be. It feels like I'll never get past this.

After all this time, I still miss you. I can't imagine a day when I won't.

Winter

You left today.

There's not much else left to say.

It wasn't a bad dream; I really lost you.

Maybe I'll never love again.

I had a bad day.

I've been having a lot of them lately.

I want to talk to someone about it but I don't know where to start,

Or even how to say it,

Or who to tell.

–Seeking a therapist

Winter

I want to shut out the world

Close the blinds

Keep the sun and air out

I want to suffocate

Not move from this place

But wallow in it

–Depression makes me closed off

Clenched teeth

Knotted stomach

Unsettled mind

Clammy hands

Racing heart

Can't sit still

–Anxiety

Some days,

I want to bury myself under a blanket

And never get up.

How is it that you can feel so happy,

And all of a sudden,

A wave of sadness

Just comes out of nowhere

And knocks you off your feet?

–*Depression hits hard*

I

feel

EVERY THING

And

NOTHING

All

at

once.

Death is inevitable and finite.

Most of us get the chance to grow old and live out our days.

You won't get that chance, and that is infinitely painful.

Even though you are gone, there's still a part of you somewhere in the universe,

Somewhere good with only incredible things.

I hope you're at peace.

Everything hurts;

I can't make it stop.

Some days are so long and challenging and achy.

Some days it really hurts just to exist.

–Mental illness is real

I am calling bullshit on the entire set of assumptions and circumstances around the "It gets better!" message. Not only is the assumption about happiness as the ultimate emotional state of being a concern; even more problematic is the dismissal of mental health challenges.

Because, sometimes, it doesn't get better. It is unfair to continue to suffer for an undetermined amount of time until the day everything magically "gets better." Though some may be lucky enough to persevere through their circumstances and reach that point, not all of us are that lucky, and it is not an excuse to not get help.

That is another problem with this claim: it can discourage those who are suffering from seeking the help that they may need if they believe that, one day, things will get better. Chances are, things do not actively get better on their own—it is usually a lifestyle change or some sort of active step taken to create a feeling or situation of betterment.

If you are struggling or feeling stuck in your life, it is absolutely okay—and should be encouraged—to seek out help and support from others.

I don't know what's wrong with me.

How can something be too much and not enough all at once?

I'll never be the same

Because you broke me.

Winter

I was so young and unprepared,

But I've moved on,

And I'm never coming back.

This has gone on way too long—

It's time to put this to an end.

So I'm going to tell you I'm leaving and never coming back.

I'm not going to fall for you anymore.

I'm not going to let you break my heart again.

I'm not going to gaze into those beautiful eyes anymore,

'Cause I'm leaving…

It is so important to allow ourselves to stop the insanity for a moment, take a step back, and just breathe. We are all human, and we are all struggling with various manifestations of life's expectations in different ways.

Being able to recognize that and, I suppose, recognizing the impossibility of being able to truly achieve *everything*, can maybe cause us to discover what is really important to us and prioritize those aspects rather than attempting to do it all.

That is something that has always been difficult for me, but I'm trying. And I know I'm not alone.

Coping with life is a lot right now.

You are allowed to feel whatever you are feeling;

it is completely valid.

If you are struggling, it doesn't mean you're failing—

it just means you're human.

We used to talk about everything under the sun, and look where we are now:

Now we walk down the halls avoiding each other's eyes.

You tried to get in touch with me a couple of times,

But after everything that happened,

I just couldn't do it.

I had to let everything we had go.

I think you now fully understand that it is either them or me;

You can't have us both.

Luckily we got some time together,

But now you're back to them

And I'm gone, gone, gone…

I've given you so many chances.

I fell in love with you, even though I never ever wanted to.

I gave it all up for you, but did you see?

No.

You still don't realize that you were my everything.

But not anymore.

I had to let you go.

It's not fair for me to live like that.

There is so much more in the world for me to explore,

And now it's time for me to go see it.

Letting you go was the most painful thing I have ever done,

But it was important.

Sometimes we need to let things go to let new things rise.

It is necessary to let go of past relationships to allow

room for growth.

Since I've let go, good things are starting to happen. Things are

finally starting to fall into place.

Even though it was hard, I know I made the right decision.

It's okay to let go of the things that cause you harm—

the things that tear you down, the things that make you feel like

anything less than your amazing self.

You owe it to yourself to pursue the happiest, most fulfilling,

authentic life you can.

I was lucky enough to know you and love you.

But I had to let you go, so you could have a chance

To get all of the things you ever wanted.

Winter

Because of them, I fucked up everything with you.

I know it will never be the same because of the choices I made.

At the end of the day, as long as we're both happy, that's all that really matters…

But they make both of us happy

And I think the easiest way for me to get out of this situation

Is to let both of you go.

It can't be the same as it was;

It's time for all of us to move on.

That was then, this is now.

Gotta keep my eyes ahead, no looking back—

Gotta push past this somehow.

No regrets—no, I'll never have them—

It was what I had to do.

Back then I thought I was in love with you,

But you see, baby, it's not true

'Cause I'm over you.

No.

You don't get to walk all over me anymore.

Take your toxic bullshit

And get the fuck out of my life.

There's only room for love in it now.

I will say my piece, and then I can move on.

I am going to do just fine

Without you.

I let you

Write the rules

For so long,

But not anymore.

I am the author of my story,

Not you.

It's my turn now.

Now it's time for me

To put the pieces that you broke

Back together

And start again.

The door finally slammed in my face, and I woke up. I could not stay on the path I was on or I would self-destruct. I had been doing it already without fully realizing it. I could no longer convince myself that I was happy with the life I was living once I got a taste of what it could be, out there, away from here.

I saw something different for myself than the path I was on at that point in time. I decided to reach for it, by making the decision to change everything. It was a really hard decision—choosing to give up everything for the possibility of something unknown is terrifying.

I was so uncertain at the time, and I questioned my decision every day. I was so scared of what the future was going to bring, and I didn't know how it was going to turn out. I just knew that I needed something different. It wasn't that I wanted something different; I *needed* it. I had to change.

Too many people (myself included) have life-changing experiences, but are too afraid to actually change their lives after it happens. I am not going to be one of those people. I have to move forward and reach for what I know I can become. I know what I want, and I will not let anything hold me back.

It finally feels like a new path has been carved out for me.

A new journey to embark on, with no more negativity or toxicity, or being held back or holding myself back.

I have let go of all of the things that were weighing me down, including those things within myself.

After all of this chaos, confusion, second-guessing, and uncertainty, it finally feels like the clouds are starting to clear. The light is starting to come in. New growth is coming.

It is time to step forward into the incredible future that I know awaits.

It is time to begin again.

Spring

Blooming: Poetry for Seasons of Change

After feeling like you haven't been yourself in awhile, it is so refreshing to finally take a breath of fresh air. After all this time, all the chaos and heartache and heaviness, it is finally starting to lift.

Starting over is a hard process. But after all of these moments, it's necessary. Starting over is not the same as giving up and it does not make you weak. It is taking your future into your hands, and creating the life that you know you deserve. It's going to be a bit messy at the beginning. But eventually, everything will fall into place.

You know that this was the right decision. You've had a glimpse of what your life can be, and you are going to go get it.

This is what starting over is like. It's a process, but you will get there.

You just need to have the courage to start.

Morocco was a whirl of excitement.

I only had four short days there; it went by so quickly that it was hard for me to fully process.

After some reflection, I have come to realize what did happen:

I became strong. I became confident and sure of myself. I grew stronger friendships by the day.

I was not afraid to be in a new place and explore. I was starting to feel like myself again—the person I had been, but somehow lost along the way.

–*Morocco*

I was excited to be travelling on my own again in Barcelona. I think that was when the realizations started to kick in. Being on your own puts things into perspective.

It was nice. I liked being by myself, making my own decisions, having faith in myself.

It was something I hadn't felt in awhile, and it felt good to know that I could take care of myself.

–*Spain*

I could feel it: walking alone in the streets of Lisbon,

Getting lost and finding my way back again.

I could feel it in the whirr of the metro and my ability to navigate the city.

Walking along the shoreline of the ocean and wading in its waters;

Looking at the view from rooftop bars and viewpoints;

Partying at Urban Beach at 4 am;

And in the burgers and ciders I had with friends.

I could feel it in brunch, I could feel it in dancing,

I could feel it all.

I had re-discovered the person I used to be,

Or better yet,

The person I was meant to be.

And I wasn't ready to let her go just yet.

–Portugal

You can rewrite your story at any time.

It's your life; you're the one who gets to create it.

This life is short. Make it worthwhile.

Even though saying goodbye means

Moving on to my next adventure,

It is still so difficult to move forward.

–Mixed emotions

I might not be okay right now, but I will be.

Perhaps soulmates are made,

Not found.

After all this time, I have come to realize one of the most important relationships I have is with myself. But after everything that has happened, that sense of self has really gotten lost along the way.

Re-discovering myself is important and necessary to move forward. I am finding it in new ways every day.

Whether it's my ability to rise to challenges that I had never imagined, creating new friendships with people that make me feel full of love and light, trying new things to continually push myself outside of my comfort zone, exploring new places at home and abroad to push my limits, finding ways to be centred amidst the continuing craziness of life… It's all part of the process.

It will take some time until I feel fully in a good place with myself, but I'm getting there. And I'm trying. And that is so much more than enough.

I've lost so many old versions of myself and gained so many new ones along the way.

I'm constantly evolving, growing, changing.

It's the only constant in life.

I am learning to enjoy where I'm at now,

Rather than anticipating what the next, newest version of me will be.

Spring

If you knew me before, we need to get re-acquainted.

I've changed so much that sometimes I barely recognize the person in the mirror.

Things I do for self-care that keep me going:

- Set clear boundaries and stick to them
- Do not overwork or work overtime unless absolutely necessary
- Take medication
- Go to counselling every few weeks
- Have regular check ins with my doctor
- Connect with others to nurture positive relationships
- Practice yoga and other forms of movement
- Go for walks, get fresh air
- Journal and write
- Surround myself with others who add value to my life
- Say no more often, especially to negative/toxic relationships
- Honour my intuition
- Maintain a healthy diet—be aware of things my body doesn't like being put into it, but allow room for enjoyment
- Allow time for rest and relaxation
- Make consistent check-ins on vital areas of life to see how things are going
- Be aware of how I'm using my time
- Use affirmations
- Practice meditation

Spring

I look in the mirror

And see god looking back at me

Even the mistakes are important

Because they've made me who I am.

You live through the failures and learn from them.

You see, we can't truly love ourselves until

We accept everything we've done;

Every single part of us—

The good, the bad, the ups and downs.

They make us who we are.

If you are looking for more ways to support your mental health, here is where to begin:

1. Start small.
2. Work your way up slowly.
3. Take it one step at a time.

–*You've got this*

I don't want to live to please others;

It's exhausting and something that can't ever be accomplished,

Because someone will always be unhappy.

Rather, I want to live for myself.

She is the only person I care about impressing

And the one who needs me the most.

The places that slowly put my pieces back together again:

- Barcelona
- Rooftop bars
- Lisbon
- Sangria-filled nights with friends
- Toronto
- Wandering the streets of a new city
- Vancouver
- Friends who become family

Let me find what you need,

Let me give you all that I can,

Let me lift you so we can both rise higher—

Level the playing field

And shatter all preconceptions of

Who they think we should be.

Things I am grateful for:

The people I have met who continually encourage me to be my best self and chase my craziest dreams

The places I have been that fill me with inspiration, peace, joy, un-comfort, strength, and love

The challenges I have overcome and all that I will continue to rise up to do

My dreams that will always get bigger and better and keep me moving in the right direction

You have gone through so much, but you don't need to keep doing it alone.

If there is a storm raging inside of you, you don't need to keep it all in.

I know it's hard, but you need to let your feelings out.

However you are feeling right now, you're not alone. I've been there.

So many of us have.

Don't be afraid to reach out for help. We all need it.

We need each other—we're all we've got.

–Reach out today

Spring

I know it all feels so heavy right now,

But it is so important that you know this:

You are not alone.

I have struggled with finding balance in the past. Chaos has a tendency to take over and things feel so complicated. I can never seem to find a way to pull it all together and feel balanced—at peace.

But lately, things have felt different. They *are* coming together. It finally feels as if things are beginning to align—falling into place.

I am choosing my own path, and with it is coming more clarity and cohesion than I ever could have imagined. This is what living a balanced and fulfilled life feels like. It doesn't mean that it's perfect. It's always a process. But it finally feels complete.

Rather than living in the past or worrying about the future,

Be present *here*

In this very moment.

Even in the chaos,

There are still moments of love and light.

All we can do

Is navigate our way through the pandemonium

And hope we make it out the other side.

"Everything happens for a reason" used to be one of my favorite phrases.

I sought to find the meaning in everything.

But, sometimes, *life just sucks.*

There might not be a reason for every shitty situation that happens.

And that's okay.

Accepting that there are some things you will never truly know, some answers you will never get, is necessary to move forward.

For without the pain, how would we know joy?

Happiness is elusive;

Perhaps we need to create it ourselves.

Things that make me happy:
- Taking time for self care
- Being healthy
- Kind strangers
- Driving alone and blasting music
- Watching Gilmore Girls and New Girl
- Exploring new places
- Yoga and spin
- Performing
- Writing
- Public speaking
- My family
- Great colleagues
- You

Spring

Home has meant a lot of different things to me

At many different points in my life.

It's something I've struggled with quite a bit in the past.

But I've come to realize that,

Sometimes,

Home is more of a feeling than anything else.

Hold on to the good things when they come your way;

You deserve it.

–Blessings

Spring

You have everything you need within yourself to make it happen.

This journey has been full of ups and downs. I am grateful for every second of it. Even the hurt, the pain, and feeling like I wanted the world to end. I wouldn't be here without any of it.

And I know that I don't have it all figured out yet—though it might seem that way. Far from it. I am continuing to figure things out as I go along. As I said, this life is a journey, and mine is far from over. I'm just getting started.

I continue to have high hopes for everything that this life will bring my way. And if you're looking for your hope—*this is it.* Have faith, gratitude, and love. It's coming; you just need to be ready and willing to receive more blessings than you ever could have imagined. It all starts and ends with you. If you are coming from a place of love and gratitude for yourself, then the rest will find you.

Spring

Everything I see

And everything I read

Is all about love—

And it's true that love

Is what makes the world go round—

Yet there are all different words of advice on

how to love someone,

Or what to do to be in love with someone,

Or how to act and in what situation, and, and, and…

It's exhausting.

Why can't we just say what we feel without worrying about the rest

of that crap?

Whatever happened to just expressing our feelings

And being honest with one another,

And seeing where it goes?

That's the kind of love advice I want to see.

–*Easier said than done*

We'll find each other in a thousand different lifetimes.

–*Meant to be*

I still don't have it all figured out yet;

I'm still finding my voice

And carving my own path.

And I don't know if I will ever fully know

Who I am, where I'm going, what I want.

But regardless, I am valuable,

And it will be okay.

It's crazy to believe that I'm finally here. It has felt like such a long road to get to this point. There were times when I didn't know if I would make it, so just being here feels like a blessing.

After all the time I've spent over the past few years, trying to run or up-level myself, or always moving on to the next best thing—I'm trying to simply sit and be content. Content is a word I'm wanting to hold onto as I head into the next phase of life. It's been a hell of a journey to get here and I don't need to push myself to do more, be more, reach for more; I can be content with where I'm at and spend some time enjoying it.

Plus, I'm just getting started. There's a lot more living to come.

Equinox

Being "happy" is this concept that I have struggled with for quite some time. It used to be so simple. I was generally a positive and happy person and it was never something that felt like it took a lot of effort for me. But somewhere along the way, things changed. Happiness suddenly felt out of reach. For a long time, I wasn't happy. I honestly couldn't remember the last time I had felt genuinely happy.

It took a long time to get back to happy. It's hard to pinpoint exactly when it happened, or how. But I do know it started with a decision to start over. That was definitely not happy at first, but my hope was that happiness was down the road somewhere. I had a strong feeling that, if I created a life that I loved and enjoyed living, happiness wouldn't be far behind.

I was right. It took a long time. For much of that time, I wanted to give up. But I held onto the hope that there was light at the end of the very long tunnel. And now I'm here. I feel on cloud nine. I have a career ahead of me that makes me feel so overjoyed and fulfilled, every single day. I have relationships that are safe spaces and bring me comfort, laughter, and love. I have carved out time in my day-to-day life to do the things that bring me more joy. It doesn't mean that I'm happy 24/7. I still have bad days. I will probably continue to have bad days for a long time. But it is no longer mostly bad days, and I am so much better than I was.

This journey is truly a never-ending process. I am so lucky to be around those who lift me up; who make me feel joy; who give me hope; who support and love me even when I have dark days, because dark days will come, and we all need a little extra love sometimes. It is my responsibility to lift them up too. To support them in whatever path they choose, to be a shoulder to cry on when they need it, to bring out the light when they feel there is none left in the world.

It is not about competition—who can be the best, who is the most successful, who has achieved the best goals, who is the happiest. We are all in a process of living, learning, loving, and growing. Supporting one another during this process is the most important thing.

Being surrounded by positive relationships in which both parties are lifting one another up is necessary to thrive. I am the luckiest to have so many of these currently in my life. I hope to continue to always lift up those who also lift me. We can succeed together, because we are all better together. A love-filled life is not meant to be lived alone—this love is meant to be shared.

When I look back on who I was many years ago, and even a few years ago, it all feels so different. I've lived through many low points: extreme struggles with depression and anxiety, issues with friends, issues of self-worth, and more. However, now I am so much stronger than I was then, and than I was simply a few months ago. I've made self care a priority and I'm restricting more people's access to me, prioritizing the friendships that feel fulfilling. It is amazing to see the growth that has taken place, and this continued growth makes me really excited about what's coming next.

I am slowly learning to love every inch of myself—even the parts of myself that sometimes I wish were never brought to light, the parts I want to hide away and never show the world. They are still important because they are a part of who I am. And though who I am is always evolving with everything that happens in this life, it is important to not only love where we are going and who we think we can be in the future, but to love where and who we are *in the now*. It is delicate and complex; soft and gentle.

Most importantly, it is a process that will continue to evolve as I do. If I want to live a life filled with love in everything that I do, some of that love has to be for me.

Blooming: Poetry for Seasons of Change

AN AUTHOR'S NOTE ON MENTAL HEALTH

With everything that goes on in the world, many folks are struggling with their mental health and can relate to the struggles you may also be facing. Community is necessary to get us through these difficult times, because we don't get through them alone. Check in on one another and know that we are stronger together.

Let's stop trying to sugar-coat varying emotional experiences and the impact they have on our mental health. It's okay to not be okay. You are not on this journey alone. You are allowed and encouraged to reach out for help.

When it hits you that you can't do it all, you have to figure out how to deal. If you're like me, you wind up having a crying sesh on your bedroom floor. If you're like me, you may also need a day to cancel plans, figure things out, and get back on track. Maybe you need more than a day. Or maybe you bounce back a lot quicker than I do and are able to pick yourself up again right away.

We all deal with these things in our own way. I am trying to learn my way and listen to that little voice inside my head and give myself time. Time to assess what I actually need. Time to figure out what to do next.

If you're feeling like something is off, lean into why. It may be a combination of everything else that is already going on, or there may be other additional factors at play. I read a great post that highlighted how each feeling we have is a messenger for us, letting us know what we need to tend to in order to achieve our best, full selves. I wholeheartedly agree and I'm trying to get in the practice more often of naming my feelings and questioning what these feelings are trying to tell me. Journaling has definitely helped me with this process.

Whichever actions, or non-actions, will bring you the most peace and fulfill your needs in this moment—do them. You are truly the only one who can decide what you need in each moment. Learning to trust yourself and listen to what your body and mind are telling you is crucial to improve your wellbeing.

There is always someone here for you—whether that is a partner, friend, loved one, colleague, mental health professional, etc. You have people to turn to who may be experiencing similar things right now.

You are not alone. Never choose to suffer in silence.

ACKNOWLEDGEMENTS

I have many wonderful people to thank for helping make *Blooming* a reality!

First and foremost, to the wonderful TSPA team, without whom this book truly wouldn't be possible! Megan, our fierce leader—I am so grateful to have started following your journey many years ago, and even more grateful to have you as a part of my own journey. Endlessly inspired by you and so happy to have you on my team! Anna, our powerful brand coach - our one session together was mighty and I think about it often. Thank you for sharing your gifts of story-telling with me! Ira, our mega-organized strategist—I truly wouldn't have been able to stick to our timelines without you keeping all of us in check, and you deserve the deepest thanks! Elise, my wonderful editor— thank you for handling this piece of my heart with so much care. It was an absolute pleasure to work together! Tracy, my fabulous designer—thank you for dealing with my many detailed notes and making my vision of what "Blooming" would look like come to life visually!

Being surrounded by a strong team of kick-ass women who know their self-publishing stuff *so* well has been inspiring! It's been a blessing to work with all of you and I know *Blooming* wouldn't have seen the light of day without your help. Thank you from the bottom of my heart. Y'all rock.

Second, to my health team for always helping me to be my best self. You have helped me get through many of the dark seasons captured in this book. I'm grateful for my wonderful doctor, who has been on my mental health journey as I discovered medication and various ways of prioritizing my mental health and well-being. My amazing therapist, who has been a part of my life journey for over three years now, has truly seen it all. We've made many leaps and bounds together. I wouldn't have had the courage to put this all together without the inner work we've done on my mental health, and for that, I'm so grateful!

Of course, I can't forget my friends and family, who didn't think I was absolutely bonkers when I said I was going to publish a book. Thanks for believing in me even when I want to do the impossible. Your support means the world. Special shoutout to K and S for being my biggest cheerleaders, and to my mom, who always said that I would be a writer — I guess you were right. Moms always are, aren't they? Love you.

And finally, to you, the reader. Thank you for picking up this book. I hope it brings you solace to know that, however you are feeling right now, you are not alone. I've been there. I know it sucks. And I also know it can get better. Never hesitate to reach out for help. I published this book for you and I hope that it brings you exactly what you need. Thank you for being a part of my journey and for inviting me in to be a part of yours.

XO,

Chiara

AUTHOR BIO

photo: Kayley Bourcier

CHIARA MASON is an author, podcaster, lifestyle blogger, traveller and mental health advocate. Through journals, song-writing, blogging and poetry, the written word has always allowed her to express life experiences and lessons. She hopes you'll find connection with her words.

You'll often find Chiara jet-setting to explore a new place, or practicing the art of wine-drinking. She grew up in the Okanagan region of British Columbia, Canada and currently lives in Toronto, Ontario. *Blooming: Poetry for Seasons of Change* is her debut collection of poetry and prose. Find more of her work at chiaragoesglobal.com.

www.ingramcontent.com/pod-product-compliance
Lightning Source LLC
Chambersburg PA
CBHW050224100526
44585CB00017BA/1927